Una Woods *was born and raised in Belfast, Ireland, where she now lives. A seminal influence on her writing was the atmosphere of the city road where she spent her early years, with its imposing three-storey terraced houses and black factory smoke and the interweaving streets where children gathered to play their seasonal games. In stark contrast to this, the other pivotal source of early awakenings was the rolling green countryside around her grandmother's house in Co Down, where she and her family spent all of the school holidays.*

After initial uncertainty about the direction her writing would take, at a certain point it became clear to her that early consciousness itself was the key to what she had to say.

' I have to keep trying to maintain the writing at the point from where I believe it originated....the effect of small light changes....the atmosphere of say the dusk falling on the city road and its implication for the whole of future life. '

Quote from **Unveiling Treasures,** *published by Attic Press, 1993.*

First published poems and short stories appeared
in the late 1970's in the New Writing Page of The
Irish Press, edited by David Marcus.
The Dark Hole Days, a novella and short stories
was published by **Blackstaff Press** in 1984.
Over the years stories and poems have appeared in
anthologies in Ireland, The UK
and USA.

Other **Una Woods** books published by **Ashtrees** are:
Afternoons, selected poems, 2006.
Mr and Mrs McKeown- the accidental maze, a novella, 2010.
An icicle for an eye, notepoems, 2011.
2 Plays, Grace before meals; For want of the call, 2013.

splintered vision

by una woods

Published by Ashtrees 2016, re-issued 2017.
Email: ashtreespress @ gmail.com

ISBN: 978-0-9575858-5-0

*To Ossian, Naoise, Oscar and Anton
with love*

The blunt of chimney
all is left of it against the dim sunk day
say hurray
the time and place is right

stop still
a language is about to be committed
forgive it its trespasses

row-stacked upward towards
the Springfield dam   say it
chimney- condemned space for its coming words
stark still dusk behind

all the road falls victim
a hung jury the only air

is that it frail-glimmered on the Black mountain
then the act goes on
once committed on

out there
where the slight wind
stirs leafy rooftops
September is a swallow
twisting in the light
that glows high
time is loosened on
red tiles like
silent wires stretched across
one wide blue sky
where swallows gathered
and down below cars going round
the roundabout caught
the same sun's gleam

                                        the idea of life
                                        then the will to the idea
                                        and how memory
                                        serves both

the street lamp
is an absolute reminder
once it stood
for nothing
on the night street

                      utterly
                      on the faint hills
                        the future-past

time
is a pretence
at standing still
catch it
in the act

                    don't go airy-fairy
                    on the purpose
                  the garden stones
                  were after all
                  more than flower-borders

Spring
can't hold a bud
to the necessary gleam
of Autumn

down the street
a moonray
on the closed club door
like inside knowledge
out on a limb

the polished incense
of chapel pews
belief paused
just inside the heavy doors
salvation balanced on the surface
of smoky wood
in the beginning
was a genuflection
at the altar of shine

the crowded dusk
is an evaporating place
to be among

brick
was too hard to stand
it had to jump off light
as if its life
depended on it

              what is there
                to be
                but ready

what
just at the point of changing
can't be changed
but is
change itself

the ragweed's yellow dazzle
couldn't save it
from the sickle's silver slice
summer's hard choice
was the gleam of both lost worlds

the sound of the corncrake
started a thought-
that the future was a secret
the suburbs buried in the bogfields

the moment you knew
it was all on the surface
and everything else
was just a facade

the single knowledge
that something had to be done
with the shock of it all

the fanlight is faint
between the trees
winter is a terraced way
houses rustle barely
 side by side
what is exposed
is nowhere to be seen

find the point of
alone
on a flagstone
don't lose it
for fear of standing
alone

the buzz
 of a bee
diminishing
stretches belief
in summer

all moods
start with the light
since the light is fundamentally
changeable

the log-fire sunset
crackling at the day's fall
the distant lull
of a smoky-sweet parlour
or the time of the day
that cuts to the bone

where the unconscious
startles the conscious
a deep clarity explodes
somewhere once been
flashes at vanishing point
utterly confirmed
a moment after

as far as you can go
into the bitter street light
once no-one is out
was the extreme of yourself
now its very centre

the blackberry bucket
gleam of late August
each world
dropped softly
hope by round hope
into
the bright bulging
abyss

the field
the joy
joy's field
nothing
but joy's word

lambs
are barren snowdrops
exiled in the cold
the extreme birth-cry of Spring
 a thin audible frost on hills
faith's furthest rock
where nothing grows
let alone little lambs

search only for words
that have silence
written all over them
between them
and apart from them

cloudless sky
like a fathomless southern sea where
no boats are in sight
here in this northern blue
today is altogether displaced
the trees are a full crackling still
parked cars drift out on a haze of gleam
the courtyard tiles throb, trapped
 under a pacific sun

like closing your upward eyes
in the high field

be released
onto the chapel steps
there are bluebells
on the Giant's foot

the monastery bell
rang out across
the weak evening streets
like a sound
only the self knew

blue wasteland
born in the splintered
vision
sight is alone
 as far as it can see
jagged pieces of bottled glint
are strewn across the daisy dump

this is the journey
the arrival
and the promised land

the leaf-bird flits
the sun-rain taps the trees
lightly known the
door-knob's slight
brass twist
talk-dotted kitchen a
spoon chips the space
of a china cup
what no-one else sees
or is all-seen
the brief pause
between two doors

absence gazed
on street walls
that time of the evening
light sucked out of itself
something that's
nothing to be done
up at the corner palpable life
 loped into view, streaked unkind shadows
 on failing flagstones

neglect this space
at your peril
a voice from a nearby street called
or silence to that effect

a sudden pause
on the big stone step
orchard trees rustled to disturb
 the future split leaf-ways
yet a moment before
the racing sun was dazzled
by a life of whitewashed walls

it might be
one word

once the fanlight fails
the test of time
there is no going back
to glimmer's first
conscious light
what saw the point of fail
and fixed it to the start
of searching high and low

the factory horn
blasted the news
there is no natural birth
and being awake
is a long noise that
shocks the silence
into asking questions that
go right to the heart
of the factory horn

even a desert
can save the day
if its sand is quick

the city screeches
like a seabird
displaced by cliff-clouds
miles from anywhere
perches on the eaves
of the afternoon
as if by chance buildings
roads and reason
could dissolve into the nature
of waves

imagine a path
petalled with the future's
fluttering air
imagine
a path the past
sets free from imagination

the road was born
in a state of original mood
concealed by the sun
and the first will to a baptised wall
fundamentally a shade
of grey

doorway dipped
in mellow song
light strung out
across the top of the field
a ladybird better
makes the case
for glitter fixed
on a frail idea
touching down
in the zone of flowers
without long gaze
or melody's time-felt mood

nipped in the bud
of winter sunlight
the fluttering Autumn leaf
is what you believe
to be the case
lightly suspended

lamplight shares its haze
with the first sign of
consciousness
there is no disputing
their dim awareness
of some illumination unrevealed

have faith in the onceness
of things   and how
origins swim and glisten
on the surface of a vast unknown

the rooftops are scathing
about the winter sky
red slate
is at the cutting edge
of cold
smoke is stripped from
the solitary chimney pots
the wind is caught in the crossfire
of sniping branches
memory is a minimalist
in an isolated moment
of awareness

nothing is itself
and each thing is itself alone
in the double life
of the image
consciousness accounts
for one   the other
is the image of it

the small gate knew
in its gritty clink
it could swing life
one way
or another
and that closed could be open
to the sound of silent footsteps

the leap of faith
of a word
paper's deceptive
clean page
empty white squawks
like a country crow
looking for elm trees
on city cement

godforsaken pier
remote end
of desolation
dabbling in the depth of the unknown
sea   meeting its maker
in the still unplumbed future
of the early eye

the sign of the dusk
light crosses itself
and puts its faith
in the imperceptible point
of change
there is a shimmer
on the roofs   slate
holds it there
the same slate that praised
the sun on high
pays homage to the last lucid moment
between day and night

the lough
finally lovely
the blue lough unseen
the cold bluster of
the outward sail
the sun breaking hard on
the grey stones
the forbidding lough
finally blue
is opening out over the rooftops
on the low-lit sail
of this city winter

those moments
when life is lived
in parallel places
to the full

moonlight
night's still plough
sits on the high field
the earth's work is suspended
on one silver end
of summer days

so to speak the things
that rush to mood's rescue
deep in a sunlit valley
a clutch of white cottages
exclaims
the thriving point
of isolated living

the morning sun
on the factory wall
had a vacancy
that needed to be filled

a word
unheard once
in the fading street
a voice is born
to utter nothing
a streetlamp shares
precious little
with this stark silence

brick had nothing to build
in the falling light
so it occupied itself
by catching the light
and cementing it
to the busy point
of fade

secrets in the galore

gloom

the night is next

to nothing   on a window

branches suspend tapping

on the twig of crooked

shadows   silence

is turned inside

out   footsteps

on the night stairs

scratch the threadbare surface

of sadness

dust of ages

on the sparse pavement

all the words

of sermons

scattered on cold tiles

a bus brakes

the schism

is concealed

but the incense is cast

the afternoon hummed
as if the whole thing
could be revealed by overhearing
the front of the road

in a fundamental time
and place
a oneness external to both
glowed
the street willed it
with a question
that deflected its answer
a ball bounced off
the gable, simultaneously
the sun

the wheelbarrow
with nothing to do
works away at idleness
and the barn door
by lying open
grasps the point
of the empty yard

privacy is
a discovered path silence twists
and turns   a stick of sunlight
pokes furtively
on the far side of the road
the nature of keeping quiet
is disturbed in the dust's
stony sparkle   a stranger
huddles close to the high wall's
hidden purpose
affirming the unspoken fear
that life will be exposed

garden stones
commandments placed around
the edge
 of the freedom of flowers to grow
 wild
or in themselves symbols
of summer's real intention
to write in stone
the fleeting perfume of
the freesia
and set it apart from the
eccentric diversions of the path

evening light delayed
on the terraced row
like an appeal lodged
for a suspended verdict

what took shape was
the reality of transience
moments of transparency
that could pass for
a way of life

what do you know
beyond that first faint signal
night's glitter on the high field
to say nothing but
there you go

.

an impression of change
lit the gable wall
until gradually
the gable wall stood
for constant change

how to go on
after the rooster's dawn crow-
believe it is one possibility
and one alone

the slow burn
of birth
sparks appear in
strange places
ashes that smoulder
in the bland morning grate
too hot to throw out
but no good to light
a fire

being as a leaf
snatches at a bus-stop
the image of who
alights   a brief breeze
on the empty pavement

an unoccupied
bus-stop on a deserted
evening road
is belief's beggar

the sun easily scoops
up the shallow water
of the careless river
just past the bend
drooped over with reeds
a pearly frog sprung
from stone   the day sits aloof
on the blue hills of summer
small voices paddle the
mid-air as if talk is all
in good time

down among
the summer streets
picking steps off
pavements
to make a bunch of being
lighthearted

in the insect-dotted light
of the sea-front window
a silhouette is washing
splashing soapy water from an
enamel bowl   a boat moves
imperceptibly across the horizon
but the silhouette is already aboard
the distant smell of seaside soap

what can't be taught
the moon's bright courtyard
face   cobblestones
that trot out a horse's early
morning measure and more
the first commandment
of a terraced row   the transient
 worship of the Friday road

and that light
hard as a brick
on the street corner
as if built
to last

already since out there
like a muffled drum
all times before beat
once a future struck out
bell-piano clear
notes in their original
black-and-white
air
Oft in the Stilly Night
repeat

footsteps on pebbles
want to go there

since machinery
the moment determined
or more generally the rattle
could be questioned
a definite sign
the face at the window
looking out as if to say
I hear the beginning
of time
or end

what appears to need
only a slight adjustment
to be its ideal self
or what it was once
when self was itself
an idea

the repetitive flap
of a sign   as if
 the windy road is intent on keeping
monotony's empty promise

foxglove
firelight
the foggy prayer
mildewed whins
on the morning mountainside
cottage
candlestick
the black city clock
evening's bereft tick
over the wall a street game
goes begging

what extreme blast
being stranded among
dandelions wild
in a crowd of time
outhouse feather ruffling
fought-over land
waste-begone
the future fields

always evening
in the evening
early winter
smoke hung with air
the path is pale
with waiting
fail is a thin stretch
of daylight's imagination
the crack in the door
of home from home

wish away
all hither of things
that inner chip
origins are weightless
things that spark
off themselves
stand back from the scene
thither the high field's haystack
was built to last
the winter

there is no crowd
on the night road
but everywhere emptiness
stands together
with alone

ajar the glimmer
dusk creeps
door to door
hall lights
tempt the outsider
but the prize is won
by the passer-by

light to roof
axe to log
starlight to earth
salt on ice
the black attack
of night sky
on winter country road

smoke-willow
evening's detail
the rut of a roof
dipped in weak sky
doors, like rough clues
to dim entrances
or quiet extensions
of what is going on
a figure emerges, lingers
in rigid pause at the end
of a path   then as if by nature
struts into the brick-hewn
shadows
the failing road is carefully drawn
to illuminate an exiled view

the low of a cow
 in the long evening
came from a place
that had no choice
but to exist once

wildflower reason
enough
the sudden field
finds fragile
nourishes it
for the wildflower's pure sake

why the same isolated images?
the cathedral bell for instance-
the need to be
in one particular chime
or chaos confined
to the distance to Derrylaghy

possibilities
are absolutes
in the first instance
they have nothing
to prove

March day
all around the bushes
snapping at season
time-fumbled clouds
light in the balance
cold's bite hollow
without winter resolve
the courtyard stares
at barren's scraped barrel
suddenly a scrap of brightness
breaks into a waking moment
and day and month and season
drop their claim on mood

the effort of evening
to drag itself
out of the light
to fail
is not an option

the fanlight is barely
the will to go on

the luminous space
of a twilit road
between moon-glistened trees
as if deep appearances
are an instant form
of all there is

and the lamb's Spring cry
from the unseen field
something so fundamental
it paralysed action

nothing could be clearer
than the robotic black and white
of the magpie
make it a rule
to observe the spelled-out
moment

net curtains knew
the future looked both ways
and the concealed road
turned back
to a dim parlour's filtered
view

somewhere along the way
birth lost its direction
and found itself
in a maze of life
looking for the back exit

ecstatic green
the hedgerow
height to footpath
shoulder nudges a bulging moment
leafy flight of step
thought thrown side to side
one quick word of greeting
with the haughty air
of knowing what to say

say one thing
that sharpens
the atmosphere
something and nothing
is at stake

bottles jingling
on a lorry
along the quiet road
some unfamiliar want
agitated the fields
contentment, once jolted
set out to follow
a receding suggestion's
shaky path

it's so self-evident
and finished in itself
any construction seems
unnecessary
and a betrayal
of its first abstract perception

utter the railings
where they ring
lamplight barely believes
a glimmer is gold
illuminate the slightest trace
the world
is a better place

the blackbird
is a born again idea
all bright beaked the best
of intentions
take that cold path, for example
fresh thought out
of nowhere
pick single crumbs of time
frost quickens to twilight
the new blackbird cleanly
vanishes

buttercups
made sense of
the sun's iron will
however lost they appeared
in the side field

disillusion's front
was two doors down
the row
what say you
who passed by
neither one thing
nor another
in the glance of your early eye

at least don't plumb
for meaning
each single word is
but that stone thrown
into the thick green pond
beyond the bridge
ripples formed a receding
reflection
of the stunned impact on the surface
a moment before

any one of these things
is but the outer image
the random shell spotted
on the empty shore
who picks it up
expects more

blithe is the bite
of the autumn air
deep sunset salmon
a cold snap of leaves
alive is a single
shot at abstract
focussed on a distant
unknown fact
glimpsed over with early winter

silver slice of hidden river
remnant ray on the slope of road
turn left
swiftly past the bible cottages
are the strangers within
or hiding in the turquoise hills?

the cow's earthy hoof
evening-sunk inside the gate
of the side field
around the countryside a width
of doubt was stamped
on coming home

a bang
in the night yard
started the idea
of complete silence

quiet low
the blue-grey fade
all exposed
the single view
private life
to November late afternoon

yet that distant birth
fragile as mankind in a
stable   a star
only a sky's throw away
wonder of gold amid
winter snow
then after a moment's
unsilent night
all but the radiant scene
dispelled

how little
in the end
to the beginning
to the end

ahead
the lane exit
the light prickling through
from the Damolly road
all you needed to know
for now

faint is far
the better glimpse
barely a breeze
still wavers the fields
what laneway pricked
the stretch of view
running, passing
through and through

what glimmer goes to say
but stops short–
the street's secret
is safe with me

the street lamp
is a faint stretch
of the evening's imagination
stolen from dusk's slightly open
door

Kenmare moment

liquid blaze
through a design of fir trees
mottled September
the chirrupy quiver
of dark leaves
kitchen sounds
dulled through a door/
off-white chinks of delft
a child's intermittent
cry-   not urgent
but wanting

          someone fails
          to answer a door once
          and the future's expectant face
          is turned away

October
fizzles in
light nips the air
there is a hint of brass
about the lulled trees
a mood of mist
sits on the invisible surface
of things
know nothing
then only remember
the bustling tinge
of being out
on the October road

the rare clear moment
like the acoustics
in the music room, singing
a choir's exiled unison

ice black
country road
silence spiked
with night words
desultory snapped up
by cold air
and turned into
a critical star
vast is on the verge
of being understood

the cold winter scene
freezes choice's extreme
at the point
of what has to be

image abrupt
bell sharp
the cause is
rung across
the chosen hills
there is one
once
and one alone

privacy peals
like a grey road
the stranger walks
the curtains are cold
the tight-lipped atmosphere of
a quiet-shaped evening
turns the key
and enters the lifetime
of an old city house's secrets

the image of being
assents to the all
of a glimpse
a view of belonging
is isolated
memory's reflected brilliance
is born in
particular premonitions
would be seen as life

possibility
is the impulse of a scene
to its memory

birds rail
against the silent dawn
the moment of waking
is broken
the world is exposed
as a crack
in the unconscious

a word
to foretell nothing
a shiny word
like void

the early conscious
saw what was
close to birth

and on the moor
bracken dares
to call out
barren's name

a thought rattles
the winter door
do it justice
let it freeze
on the doorstep

the thinned-out blue
of the winter road
was a sign
that empty was a means
to one transparent day

real
is a hard dazzle
on everyday things

footsteps
know pebbles
by heart

the shop light
time's spendthrift
the moon
a silver coin slipped
in night's pocket
a sound
steals a moment
from silence   and still
there is something else
going on

gleaming sail
of a brass letterbox
bay window swum
in sun-shadows
the ideal departure's
arrival's departure
struck home

pump froth
cool squelch
orchard prickles
sun-leafed days
voices jump
over shadow stone
mould perfection
to its place
don't speak outside
the white-washed wall

steeple sky
tapered truth
up to time
will tell
adrift the blue
the steepled sky
narrows down belief

a thought
like a cat's eyes
luminous
unattached
staring night
in the face

lamb of the field
who takes away the world
with a ghost-child's cry
a terrible twilight
over the townlands
lights the wilderness
of birth

vague
vacant
lamplight
the law of the street
suspended

anyone can be
a shadow on the road
half-inclined
to a path where the light
is half-way to dark
slips in to the sound
of a key the street light
sheds dim on the
closed door

instead of saying
nothing   the bluebells
dazzle in the deepest
wood
but the word blue
is an isolated winter bloom

look at the wind
on the hedgy wall
and the primitive sun
spared of all
knowledge
but one

the word, like origins
essentially
in the air
urgently calling out
what can't be heard

crows crack at
high staggered light
the tall trees snap
or wind wastes the air
noise edges silence out
to sharpen time
and still the road
opened on and round
to the bridge over the Clanrye river
being the prize

the big yard
cut with cowshed
sun the hayloft
tickles space
with a musty sweet smell
the will to summer
is ajar   across the
dunghill a shade of
trees holds back   imperceptibly
memory makes its move

Beara Peninsula
April 2015

What stills
in its vast retreat
Atlantic glass turquoise
shimmers in from
an infinite horizon

far beneath the silent garden
gannets dive
single white life-snippets
repeat

centuries like waves of
feathers curl around
the time-chiselled peninsula

appearing out of the vivid blue
as if on memory's glinting raft
this one day unfolds

the evening bus
whipped up
a flurry of dust
caught the sun
on a kerb
and the eye
of a future waiting
passenger

who came
into the street
at this late hour?
hoping for a sign
of early life

the five o'clock
city road
early autumn sun rustles
 on a glass bay
above and beyond
the light is busy with
 an air of surprise

the novena bell
left the city
in disbelief
door to terraced door
fanlights flickered
like candles lit
to eternity
leaning over his gate
one man made small talk
with any living soul
to pass the long evening

up on the horizon
tinkles of sun
hit the pavement
music notes, like small black birds
soar in a leather
music case
carried with care
lest a piano should disappear
between two houses

what's the matter
with the light
sucked in
by the grey sky
as if infinity fails
at the first attempt

moody sea- sky
stones city grey
built up along
the kerb of the busy water
a seagull washed
high by the wind
screeches like a
new-born child leaving
an ice-cream stall
sees the colour and shape
of summer melt in her hand

the church bell
was greeted
by silence

the thought
of standing
in the lamplit street
without being seen
to remember it

buses and cars
believe the road
is rush-hour
driven
they pass by
the grass bank where a soundless
squirrel
is scampering home with a nut
for tea

how many words
to prove the inability
of words to add up
to what
the answer is
subtraction

a chimney pot
against the darkening
sky
is one reason
why

slip in
to the sound
of the afternoon
what in itself
is a source
being is
possibility and vice versa
once and for all
the world is heard
at a remove

before the road
split many ways
it caught sight
of itself
coming over the
brow of the city hill
a brilliant sun going
down behind the Black mountain

close to the main road
shadows swish
under tall Spring trees
like nuns going about
their business in an austere
convent corridor
something between the world
and a vow of silence
young green leaves
turned in a book
in the school library
the stirrings of an enclosed order

the night is on
a knife-edge
infinity is a fine
line not yet
discovered
at the end of
a noise

the ideal appeared in a rush
at the just opened door

at dusk's grainy glow
a figure times the street
to perfection
standing at the corner
flicking fade from
the fingertips of
the future

the whistle of a train
in a country town station
a blade of grass
between the thumbs
of freedom

the steady solitary clump
of homebound cows
like the earth's clock
on the dot of evening

when a murmur
 of road was not
yet separated from
the self and a
chimney pot chimed
with the sky's blue
consciousness
had no choice to make
to be free and torn
between the two

a shadow moves into
the lamp-slant of a street
 is lit by the first
light seen
on a landscape's horizon

everything changed
when a metal bin-lid was dropped
in a city night yard or
 a thrush fired song
into the suburban evening mist
the sound of the future met
the point of no return

a voice dropped
like a time-pin
in an empty place
or the road
just coming night
where someone called out
and silence took an age
to answer

listen to the surface
of the afternoon road
traffic skates
on an air of confidence
as if the thrill of things
has practised on
thin ice   until
ephemeral life becomes
the perfect performance

a bee makes small-talk
at the open door
of the summer house due
for demolition

a country yard
full of ideas
a cowshed
milking a sunray
a barrel of afternoons
rolled out on fine stones
life, depending on how
you look away from
the slightest change
in the atmosphere

shingle
for sake of
width crunching
the glistening shore
footsteps expectation
turns to hung moments
on the far side of
the bay houses mingle
in a pink ice-cream sun
or there is another reason to
look back at the approach
of the unknown sea

Scarva

Where is Scarva?
the final whistle blown
on the city in early July
the guard's shrill signal to go
one last train door bang
the carriage's stuffy dust sweetening
steam chug to quickening shunt
past the hedge-cut man
on into the countryside
fields hurtle, cows dapple the hills
mist into familiar mounds
further and closer is a house
tucked back in grey sun-hewn walls
where garden flowers go wild for
scatterbrained paths and
bees hum in the swarm of an ivied door-

summer started
with a short stop
in a small station
called Scarva

star grit
in the city's eye
above the factory roof
prickling the night view
whispering
in a dusty doorway
constellations tossed about
across the road
Mr Corscadden turned
the sign of his shop
to closed   then
the light went off

night
is the effort
of stars
to go it
alone

crab apples
took an outsider's view
of the orchard

the road is on the cusp
of contradiction
twilight winks at dusk
a front door opens privacy
then shuts it with a bang
street lamps wax dim
a figure stands
promptly on the tenterhooks
of an appointed corner

once imagining
the story alongside
steps on the silk-
lit street tripped
from one to the other
balancing houses, a luminous
moon, the future
when life would become
the finished dream

                              cowslip
                              just the name

the stations
of the cross
brought home
and laid out
agony by agony
in the street lamp's
blood-yellow
betrayal through
a window-blind

in the terraced street
the soapy scrub
of a front-door step
perfected the point
of no entry

lamplight
on the courtyard
can only mean
one thing
otherwise
there's nothing

the young trees
are frisky today
they have Friday
in their foliage
a magpie arrives
like an office-worker
collecting his pay
there is a fundamental
mood of freedom in the
scuttling sunshine
everything points to Friday
someone gets off a city bus
carrying the illusion
in a paper bag

sunlight
polishes daylight
so it can bask
in its own reflection
glory to the earth below
an unexpected bonus

things balance
on disappearance
as if their images
depend on it

ages rumble
on the country road
an old cart
carrying apples
to store in a winter cupboard
children know how far
sound travels
and carry on shaking
the orchard trees

what willed
the failing street
to rise to the view
night is a canvas
for life to draw shadow
and a stroke of moonlight
traces brick back
to the beginning of creation

burrow into
the Spring air
rake the fire
with a feather
forage through knowledge
with a blade of grass
feel time's transparency
like water tickling
the river's ankles

the street is high
on closed doors
the pavement is completely
off its flagstones
beneath the lamp
light slurs its definition
dusk's inebriated state hangs
above the rooftops
early mood experiments
with wild ideas
not knowing memory is already
becoming addicted

in moonlight's detached gaze
blue roof-slate
balances on the surface
between two worlds
and old chimney pots
hold tight to
letting go

suddenly
across the silence
of the evening countryside
a sheep cries out
from an unseen field
like the whole point
of the pointless

the long glimmer
of the dusk road
is the other side
of things
or the road is endless

the night
is spot lit
on the bend
of the road
 trees shimmer
like dancers on infinity's
stage
is tarmac's moment to
shine

a bullfinch's breast
is bursting with song
on the top branch
of the road   except
no bullfinch is seen
and the song is the
march of factory boots
released into the pink plump
landing on the hill
of the setting sun

at any taken moment
the parlour fell bare
of expectation
dust on the top
of the paused piano
scoffed at the sun
weakened through net
curtains
ashes in the afternoon
grate, pale and stricken
as if no fire on earth would burn
with fervour
while music had found
a fake note in the practised air
and returned to its natural rhythm

flagstones
the firmament
sparkles in cracks
of dust
a word spoken on the parting step
silence claims its victory
turning a key
in the vast lock
dusk's rose blooms
briefly on a road
any desert would be proud of

strange
how things happen
school books rustled
like water under the bridge
out through the corn field
was a bright yellow country
whistling on a page   still no-one
knows any better

only when things
dance with the
contradiction of
origins
like the moon's liquid blue
thrilled to be made
of street slate

                              moods
                              are in charge
                              of contradictions
                              and light is the switch
                              for mood

copper beech
an air bustling with
footsteps
pavements sink like
city sand-dunes
the low sun-glow
is a concoction
the past makes permanent
what starts out as a scene
fragments
people are watched
walking on twilit ropes
silhouettes that balance a moment
gleam starkly on the deepening rise
the fading light is a safety net
that flutters over the abyss
premonitions murmur in disbelief
at life's amazing act   then
set out to imitate it

through the skylight
a surprise of stars
like city night birds
chirping at the void

what is the point
of disappearance
is really the possibility
of the start of one time
an image like the haze of heat
grass plucked on the high field
time's invisible harp
held the strings

street lamp
the essence of things
glimmer itself
needs no light shed on it
it hangs by its own
free web through which
the street is seen

a shriek of whins
on the blast of mountainside
the sun smiles on the pearly front
of the white cottage
which is the truth?
or a voice that brushes shadows
away from the half-door

the sun
hits off a wall
and shatters
into little sharp points of view
that catch the sunlight
before being swept up by
the surging speed of the road
still
shards stray into things and
distance is cut from
the first wonderings of the
squinting sun that broke the frown
 of the city wall

the seagull
on the rooftop
is heard like the waves
of a wild sea
and desolate is the quiet road
that looks to them for comfort
instead of listening to the way to be
utterly alone

on Connolly's hill
a tractor whirrs
a reedy whistle
plays along
with the piping river
the air is a string breeze
that stirs the ears of corn
what separates and stretches
into listening spaces
hilly harmonies, lanes
where the sun jingles on
briar-berried hedgerows

summer gathers what can't be grasped
and composes itself
as if each piece
is its complete air

the effort
of the shop light
to be the business

see how
things change
what is substance one moment
bounces off another
the next
to become the scattering
image of itself–
think of the crystal sky
splintering through the ash trees

landscape
arid brick
void bedewed
the rock sun
split the upper road
survival appeared
to celebrate alone

the crocus is
a bleak little flower
that turned its back
on Crocus Street

go to say
what vanishes
close to becoming
its word

once twilight
gasped at the snowy road
the startled countryside fell
deep in pause
width listened out
 voices gloved in frosted air
sounded like questions
wrapped in answers

fade lit
the empty road
ahead to the odd
figure on the hill
life's solitary appearance
had found its belief
just in time

pause
on the front step
look up the dim
sun-dusty hall
a lifetime hangs
on the story of
a coat-hook

it's always mid-way
dandelions on the bank
prised open by the sun
to dazzle
swallows soar
by a slender margin
through a slit
in the garage door
knowing only their own
width   the smallest
weight and measure of things
the light and shape of
a moment
flies through a gap in time
as if fleeting is
a permanent abode

isolation
is a word
that glistens
once its image
appears
on the empty landscape

extremes
are self-sufficient
at their source
the light
at the top of the road
distanced itself
from being known
and was seen henceforth
as shining distance

snatches of infinity
cause of itself
imperfections the eye
can't deny
look
stand back
pass by

www.ingramcontent.com/pod-product-compliance
Lightning Source LLC
Chambersburg PA
CBHW060132050426
42448CB00010B/2088